ZHOU LONG

A Set of Chinese Folk Songs

For Solo Violin

小提琴独奏

中国民歌组曲

周 龙

MUSIC DEPARTMENT

OXFORD

UNIVERSITY PRESS

A Set of Chinese Folk Songs for Solo Violin (unaccompanied) 12' (arr. by Zhou Long)
中国民歌组曲 小提琴独奏（无伴奏）[12 分钟] 周龙改编

1) Lan Hua Hua (Shaanbei) 兰花花（陕北）：The story of a country girl who flees with her lover to escape from a forced marriage to a rich family. [about 1'30"]

2) Driving the Mule Team (Shaanxi) 赶牲灵（陕西）：As a team of mule drivers passes by, a young man looks to see if his girlfriend is among them. The melody, typical of Shaanxi style, has many fourth and minor seventh intervals. [about 1'30"]

3) The Flowing Stream (Yunnan) 小河淌水（云南）：Seeing the moon above and the flowing waters below, a young girl turns to thoughts of her lover. The rising moon is bright, my sweetheart is in the deep mountain, he is like the moon walking in the sky. My sweetheart! The flowing stream around the mountain is clear. The moon is shining over the hillside. Looking at the moon and thinking of my sweetheart, the breezes are sweeping past the hillside. My sweetheart! Don't you hear my cry? [about 1'39"]

4) Jasmine Flower (Jiangsu) 茉莉花（江苏）：Jasmine flower, such a beautiful flower, her sweet scent covers all others in the garden. I want to pluck her for myself, but I'm afraid of the garden's keeper. Jasmine flower, such a beautiful flower, she is as white as snow when she blooms. I want to pluck her for myself, but I'm afraid of gossips. Jasmine flower, such a beautiful flower, her beauty defeats all others in the garden. I want to pluck her for myself, but I'm afraid that she won't bud in the year to come. [about 1'35"]

5) A Horseherd's Mountain Song (Yunnan) 放马山歌（云南）：Folk songs are often about the mundane occurrences of everyday life. A horseherd sings about horses needing to feed on grass and the grass needing the morning dew to grow. [about 1'15"]

6) When will the Acacia Bloom? (Sichuan) 槐花几时开（四川）：A young girl awaits her lover under the Acacia tree. When asked by her mother what she is doing, she becomes embarrassed and replies that she is waiting for the Acacia flowers to bloom. [about 1'20"]

7) A Single Bamboo Can Easily Bend (Hunan) 一根竹竿容易弯（湖南）：The tune is composed in typical Hunan folk style. The words imply that unity is strength. [about 1'28"]

8) Leaving Home (Shanxi) 走西口（山西）：A wife bids farewell to her husband who is going westward to seek livelihood. [about 2'00"]

1. LAN HUA HUA
兰花花

Solo Violin

trad. SHAANBEI arr. ZHOU LONG

《陕北民歌》周龙编曲

about 1'30"

OXFORD UNIVERSITY PRESS, MUSIC DEPARTMENT, GREAT CLARENDON STREET, OXFORD OX2 6DP

2. DRIVING THE MULE TEAM
赶牲灵

Solo Violin

trad. SHAANXI arr. ZHOU LONG
《陕西民歌》周龙编曲

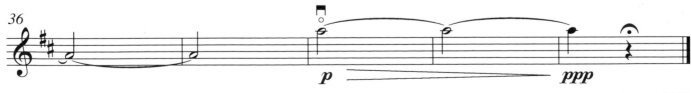

about 1'30"

3. THE FLOWING STREAM
小河淌水

Solo Violin

trad. YUNNAN arr. ZHOU LONG

《云南民歌》周龙编曲

about 1'39"

4. JASMINE FLOWER
茉莉花

Solo Violin

trad. JIANGSU arr. ZHOU LONG
《江苏民歌》周龙编曲

Slow

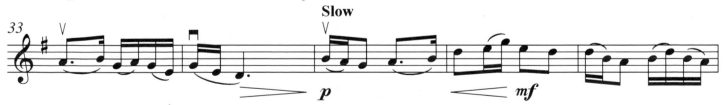

rit.

about 1'35"

5. A HORSEHERD'S MOUNTAIN SONG
放马山歌

Solo Violin

trad. YUNNAN arr. ZHOU LONG

《云南民歌》周龙编曲

about 1'15"

6. WHEN WILL THE ACACIA BLOOM?

槐花几时开

Solo Violin

trad. SICHUAN arr. ZHOU LONG

《四川民歌》周龙编曲

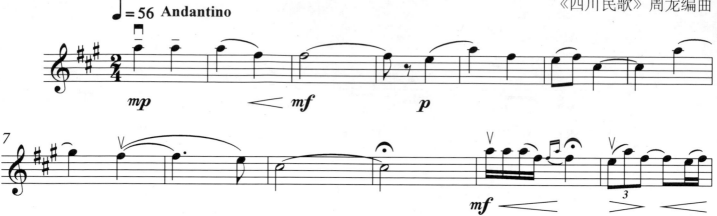

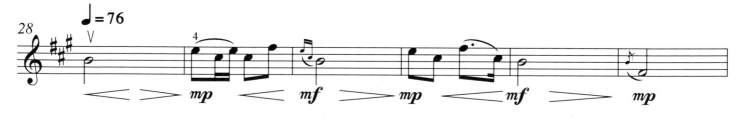

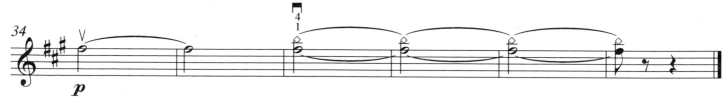

about 1'20"

7. A SINGLE BAMBOO CAN EASILY BEND
一根竹竿容易弯

Solo Violin

trad. HUNAN arr. ZHOU LONG

《湖南民歌》周龙编曲

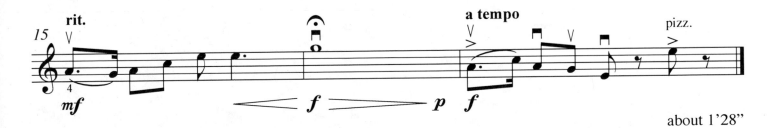

about 1'28"

8. LEAVING HOME
走西口

Solo Violin

trad. SHANXI arr. ZHOU LONG
《山西民歌》周龙编曲

about 2'00"